ASSIMILATION
OF IMMIGRANTS
IN THE MOSAIC LAND

By

Rev. Dr. Victor Fakondo Sr.

STUDIO
OF BOOKS
THE SPACE FOR YOUR MESSAGE

STUDIO OF BOOKS
THE SPACE FOR YOUR MESSAGE

Studio of Books LLC
5900 Balcones Drive Suite 100
Austin, Texas 78731
www.studioofbooks.org
Hotline: (254) 800-1183

Ordering Information:
Special discounts are available on quantity purchases by corporations, associations, and others. For details, contact the publisher at the address above.

Printed in the United States of America.

ISBN-13:   Softcover   978-1-970283-08-2
            eBook   978-1-970283-09-9

DEDICATION

To my late wife, Audrey Ann Fakondo, this book is also dedicated to you. Your love, guidance, and spirit continue to profoundly influence my life. Though you are no longer with us, your values are woven into every word. Every achievement, and every page of this book, carries your essence and spirit. Your legacy lives on, and I am forever grateful for the impact you had on our lives.

To my deceased parents, although you are not here to witness this, your love, wisdom, and encouragement have shaped me into the person I am today. This book is a testament to the values you instilled in me, and I honor your memory through this work.

To my adopted Mother: Mama Celia Davis-Fynn Davis, in Sierra Leone your unwavering support and love have been my guiding light. Your belief in me kept my passion alive, and your presence has been a constant source of encouragement. I am deeply grateful for your incredible support.

To Bishop Dr. Evans Glover of Shiloh Gospel Ministries and Bishop Dr. Lucy Anthony of the Healing Church in Maryland, and a cross-section of the membership of Bethel United African Church, as well as the African community in the diaspora, your friendship and faith have given me strength in times of challenge. To Mr. Josephus Nyandebo, Rev. Dr. Joseph Massaquoi, Senior Pastor: Rev. Christo Kamara and members of St Paul's Victory Christian Assembly in Mattapan, Massachusetts, Daniel Kurneh Allen, Mr. Joseph Lansana Jasabe, and St. Paul's Victor Christian Assembly members in Boston, Massachusetts. The Fakondo, Gulama, Bendu, Brima, Kabia, Jonjo, Foray Vandy, Thomas, Mansaray, Kanu, The Ndulue, Kabineh, Bangura, Koroma, Young all of Bethel and Lomba family. My brothers, Jonathan Fakondo in London, Michael

Fakondo in Gambia, Prince Fakondo, Simeon Bendu in Sierra Leone Emily, and Abigail in New Brunswick. Your confidence in me and my work has truly been a blessing.

To the publisher, I am profoundly thankful for your invaluable assistance in bringing this book to life. Your expertise, encouragement, and unwavering support have been instrumental in this creative journey. You helped me transform my ideas into reality, and for that, I am deeply grateful. Your contributions have left an indelible mark on both this work and my heart.

To everyone who believed in me and supported me through the writing and publication, I thank you from the bottom of my heart. Together, we have created something that will nourish the souls of many.

With deepest appreciation,

Rev Dr. Victor H. Fakondo Sr.

REV DR. VICTOR H. FAKONDO SR.- AUTHOR OF IMMIGRANTS ON THE SOCIAL ASSIMILATION IN THE MOSAIC LAND

Rev Dr. Victor H. Fakondo Sr. is a seasoned leader with a passion for faith, community service, and spiritual guidance. With over 23 years of experience as a pharmacist and a remarkable academic background, Dr. Fakondo holds multiple degrees, including a Master of Divinity in Theology, a Master of Business Administration (MBA) with a specialization in Healthcare Management, and a Doctor of Business Administration. Consultant Pharmacist from the Joint Board of Rutgers University College of Pharmacy and New Jersey Pharmaceutical Association.

In 1999, Governor Christine Whitman awarded him an award for volunteering during her inauguration.

In 2002 was featured in the New Jersey Home News Tribune for his outstanding contribution to the African Immigrants. In 2003, he was awarded the Wanda Memorial certificate by Donna Brazile of The CNN network in deep appreciation and recognition of his commitment to the mission of the Community Action Program. In the 2004 edition, he was listed as a member of the National Register "WHO's WHO's executives and professionals.

On March 30th, 2008, the Hamilton Street Business Community Corporation in Franklin Township, New Jersey, received a commendation and praise for its extraordinary contribution to creating the Hamilton Street Business District.

On April 28th, 2008, Saint Peters University Hospital, during its 100 years awarded Dr. Victor Fakondo the "Volunteer Service Award" for outstanding performances and lasting contributions to the Hospital.

On April 30th, 2008, he was awarded the NOSLINA (National Organization of Sierra Leoneans in North America special recognition award for dedicated service to the Sierra Leone community in New Jersey as an advocate, Humanitarian Activist, church leader, and Change agent who benefited hundreds of Sierra Leoneans and other disenfranchised individuals in his community.

In 2017, the Sierra Leone community of New Jersey awarded him the certificate of appreciation for outstanding community service in recognition of outstanding community service to the Sierra Leon community of New Jersey on Sierra Leone's 56th Independence anniversary.

Currently, he is the Senior Executive Director of Marie's Allied Health and Technical Institute, established in 2005, training students in the following Certified Nursing Assistant, Home Health Aide, Pharmacy Technician, Central Sterile Technician, EKG, Phlebotomy, Medical Billing, and Coding. Medical Assistant, Dental Assistant, GED, etc.

Also, the Presiding Clergy of Bethel United African Church, Inc since 2014 to date.

To God be the glory, and remarkable things He has done. My guiding angel, God, I thank You for the gift of life and for sustaining me throughout this journey.

This book, Assimilation of Immigrants in the Mosaic Land is dedicated with deep gratitude to my beloved wife, Viola Fakondo, and my children, Christiania, Victor Jr., Vernon, and Vidal. Viola, your unwavering support, patience, and understanding have been my foundation. Without you, this journey would have been incomplete. Thank you for being my guiding light and my inspiration. Your love and belief in my vision have been invaluable through the writing of this book.

To my wonderful family and siblings near and far, your encouragement and understanding have been the pillars that held me together during this process. I am forever grateful for your support.

Dr. Fakondo's journey is deeply rooted in his commitment to uplifting others through both his profession and ministry. He has been recognized on national and international platforms for his unwavering dedication, receiving prestigious awards such as commendations from President Bill Clinton for community partnerships and a service award from President Fidel Ramos of the Philippines in 2006 for strengthening bilateral community relations. 2008 The Russell Berrie Foundation was recognized as an "Unsung Hero". Recently, Dr. Fakondo was honored with an Honorary Doctorate from MEB College and the United States Presidential.

Lifetime Achievement Award from President Joe Biden, a testament to his lifelong commitment to serving others.

Motives and professionalism. In 2007, he was featured in the state Star Ledger Newspaper as "In the Spirit, "helping African immigrants in the diaspora assimilate into the system.

In 2008 the Hamilton Street Business Community Center (HSBCC) commendation and praise for his extraordinary contribution in creating the Hamilton Street Business District.

On April 28th, 2008, during Saint Peter's University Hospital's 100th anniversary, he was awarded the Volunteer Service Award for outstanding performance and lasting contributions to service.

On April 30th, 2008 Rev. Fakondo the National Organization of Sierra Leoneans (NOSLINA) awarded his special recognition for dedicated service to the Sierra Leon Community in New Jersey as an advocate, Humanitarian Activist, Church Leader, and ''change agent that benefits hundreds of Sierra Leoneans in North America In 2019, the Mayor of Jerusalem awarded him the "Jerusalem Pilgrim Certificate " certificate for fulfilling their biblical calling as he ascended to Jerusalem, the holy city and capital of Israel.

TABLE OF CONTENTS

INTRODUCTION

The United States has always been a nation built on the promise of opportunity, and its identity is, in many ways, shaped by the diverse waves of immigrants who have crossed its borders over the centuries. From the early settlers seeking religious freedom to the laborers who built the railroads to the scholars, doctors, and entrepreneurs of today, immigrants have been integral to the American story. Yet, as the country has evolved, so has the question: To what extent should immigrants be expected to assimilate into American society? More importantly, how do immigrants navigate the process of assimilation, and what does it mean for both them and the communities they enter?

In the United States, a country often advertised as a "melting pot," the question of assimilation has been debated for generations. In theory, assimilation refers to the process by which newcomers adjust to their host country's cultural norms, values, and social structures. In practice, however, assimilation is often seen as a delicate balancing act—immigrants must retain parts of their own identity while simultaneously adapting to the dominant culture of their new home.

For many Americans, the idea of immigrants assimilating into the broader culture is both a source of pride and a point of contention. Some believe that assimilation is essential to the cohesion and stability of the country, while others view it as an unnecessary demand that undermines the diversity that has made America unique. At the heart of this debate lies the fundamental question: To what extent should new arrivals embrace American ways of life, and how can they do so without losing the essence of who they are?

For immigrants themselves, this process is far from simple. While many come to the United States seeking better opportunities, safety, and freedom, they often find themselves navigating a new world where cultural norms, language barriers, and social expectations can create feelings of isolation. Yet, as time passes, many immigrants learn to adapt and thrive in their new environment, building bridges between their cultural backgrounds and the American way of life.

THE IMMIGRANT EXPERIENCE: A PERSONAL JOURNEY OF ASSIMILATION

Rev. Dr. Victor H. Fakondo Sr., a Sierra Leonean immigrant who moved to the United States in the 1980s, is a powerful example of what it means to assimilate into American society while maintaining a strong connection to one's roots. My journey reflects the broader experience of many immigrants who, despite facing initial challenges and cultural shocks, find ways to succeed and give back to their communities.

My story begins in Sierra Leone, where he was raised in a family that valued education and hard work. When he arrived in the United States as a young man, he faced the usual obstacles— language barriers, culture shock, and a lack of financial resources. Yet, through determination and the support of his fellow immigrants, Fakondo navigated these challenges and built a life for himself in the United States. He pursued higher education, earning a degree in pharmacy, and soon found himself in a position to help other immigrants like him.

But Fakondo's contribution went beyond just his success. He became a mentor and a leader in the local Sierra Leonean community, helping new immigrants adjust to life in America. Through his work at Bethel United Church, Fakondo became a pillar of support for those who needed guidance, whether it was finding housing, filling out immigration forms, or simply offering a listening ear. His story illustrates the importance of community in the assimilation process. For many immigrants, the journey to becoming "American" is not just an individual effort but a collective one.

THE ROLE OF LANGUAGE IN ASSIMILATION

One of the most obvious markers of assimilation is language. Language is a powerful tool that enables immigrants to connect with the broader society, form personal and professional relationships, and access vital services. Learning English is often seen as a key step in becoming fully integrated into American life, but this process is not always straightforward.

For immigrants who arrive from non-English-speaking countries, the challenge of learning a new language can be daunting. English is complex, with irregular spelling, idiomatic expressions, and a wide range of dialects and accents. Yet, as studies have shown, younger immigrants tend to learn English more quickly than their older counterparts. This generation of younger immigrants has the advantage of entering an environment where English is the dominant language and where schools, workplaces, and community centers provide opportunities to practice and improve their skills.

In the case of Fakondo, his English proficiency improved rapidly after arriving in the United States, though he still faced moments of discrimination due to his accent. However, as his command of the language grew, so too did his ability to navigate American society. He was able to engage more fully in his education, build relationships with his peers, and eventually establish a successful career in pharmacy. His experience mirrors that of many immigrants who, despite initial challenges, achieve fluency in English and use it as a tool for success.

EDUCATION AND THE PATH TO ECONOMIC MOBILITY

Education is another critical aspect of the assimilation process. In the United States, education is seen as the key to upward mobility, and immigrants who can access higher education are more likely to achieve economic success. Fakondo, for example, understood the importance of education from an early age, and he strongly encouraged other members of his community to pursue educational opportunities.

His story highlights a key point: many immigrants, even those who arrive with little formal education, see education as the most reliable path to success in America. They often encourage their children to pursue higher education and push for self-improvement in ways that may not have been possible in their home countries. Over time, these efforts contribute to their economic mobility and integration into the larger society.

However, the road to education is not always easy. Many immigrants face barriers such as financial constraints, unfamiliarity with the educational system, and a lack of access to resources. Nonetheless, the fact that Fakondo and others like him were able to overcome these barriers speaks to the resilience of immigrants and their determination to succeed in a new land.

THE ECONOMIC CONTRIBUTIONS OF IMMIGRANTS

The economic impact of immigration is often a point of contention in public debates. Critics argue that immigrants place a burden on public services, while proponents emphasize the positive contributions immigrants make to the workforce, economy, and innovation.

Fakondo's journey exemplifies the economic contributions that immigrants can make to their communities. As a pharmacist, he contributed to the healthcare system, and through his work with community organizations and local businesses, he helped create jobs and support economic development in his area. He also encouraged others in his community to pursue careers in healthcare, technology, and other fields, helping to build a more prosperous immigrant community.

Moreover, studies show that immigrants often bring valuable skills and diverse perspectives that can drive innovation and growth. Many of the most successful companies in the United States were founded or co-founded by immigrants, including Google, Tesla, and Intel. These entrepreneurial efforts not only create wealth for immigrants themselves but also generate economic benefits for the broader society.

CULTURAL IDENTITY AND SOCIAL INTEGRATION

While assimilation is often associated with adopting American customs, it is important to remember that immigrants do not entirely discard their cultural heritage. Instead, many adopt a hybrid identity, blending elements of their home cultures with those of their new country. This process of cultural integration is often referred to as "biculturalism," and it allows immigrants to maintain ties to their homeland while participating fully in American society.

Fakondo, for example, continues to maintain strong ties to Sierra Leone through his work with the local Sierra Leonean community. At the same time, he has embraced the values and traditions of his new home, becoming an active member of his church and community. His story demonstrates how immigrants can preserve their cultural identity while also becoming integral parts of American society.

THE ROLE OF RELIGION IN IMMIGRANT ASSIMILATION

Religion often plays a significant role in the lives of immigrants, providing a sense of community, belonging, and support. For many immigrants, religious institutions serve as an anchor during the difficult process of adapting to a new culture. Fakondo's involvement in Bethel United Church is a testament to this role. The church not only provided him with a spiritual foundation but also served as a gathering place where he could connect with others from his country and help them navigate the challenges of life in America.

Religious communities, such as the one Fakondo helped build, often serve as support networks for immigrants, offering practical assistance with issues such as housing, employment, and legal matters. These churches, mosques, and synagogues also provide a space for immigrants to celebrate their cultural traditions and pass them on to the next generation.

THE CHALLENGES OF ASSIMILATION

Despite the many benefits of assimilation, the process is not without its challenges. Immigrants often face discrimination, whether obvious or subtle, that can hinder their integration into American society. For those who do not speak English fluently or who have accents that mark them as "foreign," the path to acceptance can be slow and difficult. In addition, many immigrants struggle with feelings of isolation, particularly if they are separated from family members or live in communities where they are a minority.

Fakondo's early experiences in the United States, particularly the challenges he faced in overcoming prejudice and culture shock, are all too familiar to many immigrants. Yet, despite these obstacles, he found ways to thrive, largely because of his strong sense of community and his determination to succeed. His story shows that while assimilation can be a difficult and sometimes painful process, it is ultimately a journey of personal growth and resilience.

CHAPTER 1
INTRODUCTION TO
IMMIGRATION AND ASSIMILATION

THE IMMIGRANT EXPERIENCE IN THE U.S.

Immigration has played an integral role in shaping the United States. Since its founding, the U.S. has been a destination for people seeking freedom, safety, and economic opportunity. Waves of immigrants—each with their distinct backgrounds, traditions, and customs—have contributed to the diverse cultural landscape that characterizes the nation today. In the early years, European settlers dominated the immigration landscape, but over time, people from all parts of the world made their way to America, particularly from Latin America, Asia, and the Middle East.

The immigrant experience in the U.S. has never been monolithic. Immigrants face distinct challenges depending on their country of origin, socioeconomic background, education level, and immigration status. Yet, they often share a common desire: to build a better life for themselves and their families. This pursuit for a new beginning, however, comes with the inevitable challenge of adapting to a new country with its language, customs, and systems of governance.

While the U.S. has long been indicated as a "melting pot"—a place where various cultures blend into one cohesive whole—the reality is much more complex. Immigrants often find themselves torn between holding on to their heritage and trying to conform to the dominant cultural norms of their new country. This tension brings us to one of the most contested issues in the ongoing immigration debate: the question of assimilation.

DEFINING ASSIMILATION BEYOND LANGUAGE AND CULTURE

Assimilation is often seen as the process by which newcomers to a country gradually adopt its language, customs, and social norms while gradually shedding or modifying their own. It is the idea that immigrants should strive to "fit in" with the host country, becoming more like the native-born population over time. However, this concept is broader than simply learning English or adopting American customs. It involves navigating the complexities of social integration, economic participation, and political engagement.

The process of assimilation is not always linear. For many immigrants, especially those arriving from countries with significantly different languages and cultures, the transition can be slow and nervous with difficulty. Some immigrants may choose to maintain strong ties to their ethnic communities, relying on family networks and cultural practices that differ from mainstream American society. Others may feel pressure to abandon aspects of their culture to succeed in a new, unfamiliar environment. The degree to which assimilation is possible or desirable often depends on factors such as age, education, language proficiency, and the presence of support networks.

From the perspective of American society, assimilation has traditionally been viewed as a pathway to social mobility and integration. Immigrants who successfully navigate the assimilation process are often able to secure stable jobs, improve their quality of life, and contribute to the broader economy. Additionally, assimilation is thought to facilitate social unity—creating shared values and norms that unite diverse populations. However, as the U.S. becomes increasingly multicultural, the notion of what it means to be "American" has become more fluid, raising questions about how much assimilation is necessary.

THE POLITICAL DEBATE: TO ASSIMILATE OR NOT TO ASSIMILATE?

The issue of immigrant assimilation has long been a point of contention in American political discourse. On one hand, many conservatives argue that assimilation is essential for national unity and economic prosperity. From this perspective, the success of the American experiment relies on a shared set of values and practices. For conservatives, assimilation is a way of ensuring that immigrants fully participate in the political, social, and economic life of the nation.

According to this view, immigration should be accompanied by an expectation that newcomers will embrace the cultural norms and political ideals of the United States. Immigrants should learn English, adopt American values such as individualism and democracy, and integrate into mainstream American life. Those who resist assimilation—whether by refusing to learn English, maintaining strong ethnic communities, or rejecting American customs—are seen as a threat to social cohesion. In this framework, assimilation is not just a personal choice; it is a necessary step in securing the long-term success of the nation.

On the other hand, progressives argue that demanding full assimilation from immigrants is an exclusionary and unjust policy. They emphasize the value of cultural diversity and argue that immigrant communities should not be expected to abandon their cultural identities in favor of a singular "American" identity. Instead of assimilation, progressives often advocate for multiculturalism, the recognition and celebration of multiple cultures within society. From this perspective, the U.S. is not just a melting pot but a mosaic where diverse communities can coexist while maintaining their unique identities.

Progressives point out that immigrants already contribute significantly to American society in many ways. They fill vital roles in the workforce, create businesses, and contribute to the nation's cultural and artistic richness. Rather than forcing immigrants to conform to a set of rigid standards, progressives argue for policies that recognize the value of cultural diversity while promoting equal opportunity for all.

This political divide has real-world implications for immigration policy. In recent years, the debate over assimilation has shaped discussions around everything from immigration reform and refugee policies to the teaching of English in schools and the protection of immigrant rights. The way that Americans view assimilation will have profound consequences for the future of immigration in the country.

THE ECONOMIC BENEFITS OF ASSIMILATION

One of the key arguments in favor of assimilation is its potential to improve the economic prospects of immigrants. Immigrants who learn English, understand American social norms, and integrate into the workforce are better positioned to succeed economically. This not only benefits the immigrants themselves but also the broader economy.

When immigrants assimilate, they gain access to better jobs, higher wages, and more opportunities for social mobility. This is especially true for second-generation immigrants, who, as they assimilate into American culture, often experience significant upward mobility compared to their parents. Their ability to navigate the language and social systems of the U.S. allows them to enter higher-paying jobs, pursue higher education, and contribute more to the economy.

Moreover, the benefits of assimilation extend beyond economic prosperity. Immigrants who assimilate into American society are better able to participate in civic life. They vote, volunteer, and become engaged citizens, all of which strengthen the social fabric of the nation. Their contributions to the economy, culture, and social institutions are invaluable, and many argue that this is the essence of what makes America strong.

The economic benefits of assimilation are not limited to immigrants. Native-born citizens also stand to gain from increased cultural and economic exchange. Immigrants often bring new perspectives, skills, and ideas that enhance innovation and productivity. As immigrants integrate into American society, they form connections with native-born citizens, fostering cross-cultural exchange that enriches the country's social and economic landscape.

THE CHALLENGES OF ASSIMILATION

While assimilation can offer many benefits, it is not without its challenges. Immigrants face numerous obstacles in their efforts to integrate into American society, especially if they come from countries with drastically different social, cultural, or economic systems.

One of the most significant barriers to assimilation is language. Immigrants who do not speak English fluently face difficulties in accessing education, securing employment, and participating in civic life. Without a strong command of the English language, immigrants are often downgraded to low-wage jobs with limited opportunities for advancement. Moreover, language barriers can create isolation and social exclusion, making it harder for immigrants to build relationships with native-born citizens.

Cultural differences also pose challenges to assimilation. Immigrants may find it difficult to adapt to the fast-paced, individualistic nature of American society. The U.S. places a high value on individual autonomy, personal success, and self-reliance, which may contrast with the values of immigrants from more collectivist cultures. In some cases, this cultural gap can lead to misunderstandings, tension, and alienation.

The emotional toll of assimilation can also be significant. Immigrants often experience a sense of loss or displacement as they try to balance their old identity with their new one. The pressure to follow American norms while maintaining ties to their cultural roots can create a sense of identity crisis, particularly for younger immigrants who may feel torn between their parents' traditions and the dominant culture.

IMMIGRATION AND PUBLIC POLICY: A PATH FORWARD

The challenge for U.S. policymakers is to design immigration policies that balance the needs of both immigrants and native-born citizens. The question of assimilation cannot be answered in simple terms; instead, it requires thoughtful policies that recognize the complexity of the immigrant experience.

One approach is to focus on creating opportunities for immigrants to integrate into American society while simultaneously respecting their cultural identities. This might include initiatives such as expanding access to English language programs, providing job training, and supporting community organizations that help immigrants navigate the social and legal systems. Policies that promote upward mobility and inclusion—rather than simply expecting immigrants to follow a particular set of norms—can help ensure that immigrants can contribute meaningfully to American society.

In addition, policymakers must consider the changing nature of immigration. Today's immigrants come from diverse backgrounds, and their needs and experiences differ widely. For instance, some immigrants may arrive with higher levels of education and professional skills, while others may lack formal education and struggle to find employment. States and communities must be mindful of these differences when designing immigration policies and support systems.

Ultimately, the goal should be to create an immigration system that encourages successful integration while respecting the cultural diversity that makes America unique. By embracing the complexities of assimilation and understanding the challenges immigrants face, the U.S. can continue to thrive as a nation of immigrants.

CHAPTER 2
LANGUAGE AS A MEASURE
OF ASSIMILATION

ENGLISH PROFICIENCY IS CRUCIAL TO IMMIGRANT INTEGRATION AND SUCCESS.

Language is one of the most visible and fundamental markers of assimilation for immigrants. The ability to speak and understand English opens the door to social integration, economic opportunity, and active participation in the cultural and political life of the United States. Without proficiency in the dominant language, immigrants face significant barriers—whether it's finding stable employment, accessing public services, or simply building relationships within their new community. Therefore, measuring how well immigrants speak English and how quickly they learn it after arriving is an essential tool for understanding the extent of their assimilation into American society.

The relationship between language and assimilation is not merely practical; it is also cultural. Language is a key vehicle for transmitting cultural values, societal norms, and social behaviors. When immigrants learn English, they not only acquire the ability to communicate but also gain deeper access to the values, social structures, and even the humor of American life. English proficiency allows immigrants to navigate schools, workplaces, healthcare systems, and the media. Without it, many of these avenues remain closed, leading to social isolation and economic stagnation.

Historically, language acquisition has been considered one of the most important aspects of assimilation, and this remains true today. For immigrants in the U.S., English is not just a tool for communication; it is a bridge to belonging. The more proficient immigrants are in English, the more integrated they are likely to become in the broader society. It also allows for upward mobility, as proficiency in the language correlates closely with income and educational achievement.

YOUNGER IMMIGRANTS LEARN ENGLISH FASTER AND MORE EFFECTIVELY.

In recent years, a notable trend has emerged: The English proficiency of new immigrants is rising, especially among younger generations. This change is not due to previous waves of immigrants gradually learning more English after arriving in the U.S.; rather, it is a result of new, younger immigrants arriving with higher levels of English proficiency from the beginning. In the past, immigrants from non-English-speaking countries often had limited exposure to English before their arrival. However, the latest generation of immigrants—especially those coming from countries like India, China, West Africa, and the Philippines—are arriving in the U.S. with a much greater command of the language.

This shift is partly due to the increasing globalization of education, which has made English the lingua franca of higher education and business worldwide. In many countries, English is taught at an early age, and as a result, many young immigrants now arrive in the U.S. already possessing a functional or advanced level of English. For instance, India, despite not being an English-speaking country in the traditional sense, has a long-standing education system where English is often the medium of instruction, particularly in urban areas. Similarly, many young immigrants from Latin American countries are now attending English-language schools in their home countries, making it easier for them to transition once they arrive in the U.S.

This increase in English proficiency is significant because it indicates a shift in the immigrant experience. While past generations may have struggled with language barriers for years, the current wave of young immigrants is entering the U.S. with much better linguistic tools, allowing for faster assimilation and integration into American society. This trend is also noteworthy because it has reshaped the perception of language acquisition. Instead of being a gradual process that takes decades to bear fruit, language acquisition is now happening much more rapidly for new immigrants, particularly those who arrive as children or young adults.

In addition to this increase in language proficiency among younger immigrants, these newcomers also tend to learn English faster once in the U.S. than their older counterparts. Research has shown that younger people generally have an easier time acquiring a second language, and this is certainly the case for many of today's younger immigrants. Many of them arrive at an age where they are still in school or early in their working careers, allowing them the flexibility and time to immerse themselves in English-speaking environments. This is in stark contrast to older immigrants, who often arrive with more limited exposure to the language and may face greater difficulty in acquiring fluency.

GENERATIONAL DIFFERENCES

A key distinction between older and younger immigrant generations is the level of English proficiency they have upon arrival in the U.S. Younger immigrants today are more likely to be fluent in English when they arrive compared to those who immigrated in earlier decades. This generational difference has profound implications for assimilation, particularly in terms of economic success and social integration.

For older immigrants, learning English is often a slow and sometimes painful process. Many of these individuals may have come from rural areas or countries where English was not part of the educational curriculum. They arrive in the U.S. with varying levels of education and may struggle to find work that matches their skills due to language barriers. In addition, older immigrants often face more significant challenges in adapting to new social norms, as their lives and social networks are more deeply rooted in their home countries. As a result, they may not engage as fully in the broader American society and often remain isolated within ethnic communities.

In contrast, younger immigrants often arrive in the U.S. with a high degree of language preparedness. Many have spent years studying English in their home countries, and some may have even attended international schools or universities where English was the primary language of instruction. This strong foundation in English makes it easier for them to integrate into U.S. society. For instance, young immigrants are more likely to enter U.S. schools where English is the primary language, facilitating their linguistic and social adjustment. They also have the flexibility to navigate different social spheres—such as peer groups, community events, and workplaces—where language proficiency plays a critical role.

The difference in English proficiency between younger and older immigrants also highlights an important trend: as the U.S. becomes home to a larger share of young, highly educated immigrants, the general level of English proficiency among the immigrant population is rising. This is a significant shift, as it not only facilitates the assimilation process for the newcomers themselves but also impacts the broader American economy and social structure.

As younger immigrants continue to outperform older generations in language acquisition, their economic outcomes will likely improve, reflecting their ability to secure better-paying jobs, pursue higher education, and integrate into American professional life. In contrast, older immigrants may continue to face economic hardships related to their slower integration into the labor market. This generational gap in language proficiency and economic mobility is one of the key factors shaping the overall success of immigrant assimilation in the U.S.

THE IMPACT OF EDUCATION ON LANGUAGE LEARNING AND OVERALL INTEGRATION

Education plays a critical role in the speed and success of language acquisition, as well as in the broader process of assimilation. More educated immigrants tend to learn English faster and adapt more easily to the social and economic systems in the U.S. This is not just because of their intellectual capacity but because of how education provides them with the tools to engage with English-speaking environments.

Education helps immigrants develop critical thinking skills, which are essential for navigating the complexities of a new society. Immigrants with higher levels of education are often more accustomed to interacting with people from diverse backgrounds and are better equipped to understand and engage in discussions about cultural norms and values. These skills help ease their transition into American life, both socially and economically.

In addition, educated immigrants are more likely to attend language programs or other educational opportunities that help them improve their English skills. Many immigrants who arrive with a high level of formal education already possess the cognitive and study skills necessary to master English quickly. Moreover, highly educated immigrants are often more confident in seeking out resources to improve their language abilities, such as enrolling in adult education programs or pursuing higher education.

However, it is important to note that educational attainment is not always directly tied to language proficiency. Immigrants with higher education may still face challenges in learning English, especially if their previous education was conducted in a language other than English. Additionally, while highly educated immigrants may be more likely to find work in professional fields, they may still face discrimination based on their accents or lack of familiarity with local idioms.

Despite these challenges, the overall trend remains clear: education and English proficiency are tightly interwoven. Immigrants who are educated and proficient in English are better able to assimilate into American society, secure higher-paying jobs, and enjoy a higher standard of living. This correlation between language and education further underscores the importance of both factors in the assimilation process.

The growing trend of better-educated, English-proficient immigrants means that the gap between immigrants and native-born citizens in terms of educational attainment and language skills is narrowing. As younger immigrants continue to outpace older generations in language acquisition and educational attainment, they are increasingly becoming a highly skilled, valuable part of the American workforce.

As the U.S. continues to attract a diverse range of immigrants, understanding the dynamics of language acquisition and educational integration will be critical in shaping effective immigration and integration policies. By focusing on improving access to educational opportunities and language learning for immigrants, the U.S. can ensure that these newcomers contribute fully to the social, cultural, and economic life of the nation.

CHAPTER 3
EDUCATION AND
ECONOMIC INTEGRATION

EDUCATIONAL ATTAINMENT OF IMMIGRANTS

Over time, the educational profile of immigrants has shifted dramatically. Historically, immigrants were often less educated than the native-born population, many arriving from countries where access to higher education was limited. However, the educational landscape of immigrant communities has changed significantly. Immigrants today are among the most highly educated groups to have ever arrived in the United States. This shift has led to the closing of the educational gap between immigrants and native-born citizens.

Since 1960, the share of immigrants and native-born Americans in their prime working years (ages 25 to 54) who hold a college degree has been remarkably similar. This trend suggests that immigrants are increasingly entering the workforce with higher levels of education, contributing more skills to the economy. For many immigrants, education has become an important tool for upward mobility and greater economic success.

The increase in educational attainment among immigrants can be attributed to two main factors. First, many immigrants already in the U.S. have pursued further education over time. Immigrants who arrived with limited formal education have gone on to acquire additional schooling, raising their overall educational profile.

Second, newer waves of immigrants are arriving with higher levels of education than those who came before them. Many of today's immigrants come from countries where educational opportunities have expanded, allowing them to complete higher levels of education before migrating.

These factors combined have resulted in a significant rise in the educational attainment of the immigrant population, marking a notable shift in their economic integration. By arriving with more skills and qualifications, immigrants are better able to contribute to the U.S. economy and find higher-paying jobs.

CHANGES IN IMMIGRANT COHORTS

One of the most important shifts in the immigrant population is the changing composition of immigrant cohorts. Cohorts refer to groups of immigrants who arrive during a specific period and share similar characteristics, such as education, age, and country of origin. The educational attainment of these cohorts has changed over time, with more recent immigrants being better educated than those from earlier waves of immigration.

Younger immigrant cohorts have become the most highly educated. This group is more likely to arrive with college degrees, and in some cases, even advanced degrees. The increase in education among young immigrants can be traced to the expansion of educational opportunities in their home countries, especially in regions such as Asia and Latin America. These countries have made significant advances in improving access to education, resulting in a larger pool of educated individuals seeking opportunities abroad.

However, changes in educational attainment are not limited to young immigrants alone. Older immigrant cohorts are also arriving in the U.S. with more years of schooling and more college degrees than past generations. This trend reflects broader improvements in education globally, where individuals of all ages are now able to pursue formal education to a greater extent than before.

The shift in educational attainment across immigrant cohorts has important economic implications. The rising education levels of immigrants, both young and old, are helping them integrate into the U.S. workforce more easily. These more educated immigrants are increasingly able to secure well-paying jobs, contribute to a variety of sectors, and help close the wage gap between them and native-born citizens.

THE IMPACT OF EDUCATION ON EARNINGS

Education is a key determinant of earnings, and this is especially true for immigrants. The wage gap between immigrants and native-born citizens has been a longstanding concern, but the relationship between education and earnings helps explain how educational attainment is influencing this gap.

Immigrants with higher levels of education tend to earn more than those without. This is true not just for recent immigrants but also for older immigrants who have pursued additional education and training. In fact, college-educated immigrants often earn wages comparable to, or even higher than, native-born workers in similar fields. The increasing number of highly educated immigrants entering the labor market has helped to close the wage gap in certain sectors, particularly for those with specialized skills.

However, while education plays a crucial role in improving earnings, the wage gap between immigrants and native-born citizens is still present, especially among those without a degree. A significant portion of the immigrant population continues to be employed in low-wage, low-skill jobs, which often require little to no formal education. This discrepancy between educated and non-educated immigrant groups is one of the primary reasons for the ongoing wage gap.

It is important to consider that the wage gap between immigrants and natives is not solely driven by education. English proficiency also plays a critical role. College-educated immigrants are more likely to be fluent in English, which allows them to secure higher-paying jobs. In contrast, immigrants without a college degree may face challenges in finding well-paying work, particularly if they have limited English skills. This sorting effect—where college-educated immigrants are more likely to speak English and work in higher-paying jobs—can distort the average wage gap between immigrants and natives.

Additionally, the recognition of foreign credentials is another factor that influences earnings. Immigrants who arrive with degrees from foreign institutions may find that their qualifications are not immediately recognized by employers or professional licensing bodies. This can force them to accept lower-paying jobs or work below their qualifications, which depresses their overall earnings. Despite this, immigrants with higher education still tend to fare better economically than those without a degree, further emphasizing the role that education plays in economic integration.

SORTING BY ENGLISH ABILITY AND COMPOSITION EFFECTS

One of the main factors contributing to the wage gap between immigrants and natives is the sorting effect driven by English proficiency. College-educated immigrants are more likely to be proficient in English, which opens opportunities for them to secure higher-paying, skilled jobs. In contrast, immigrants who do not have a college degree are more likely to struggle with English proficiency, limiting their job prospects and lowering their average earnings.

This sorting effect is crucial for understanding why the wage gap between college-educated immigrants and native-born citizens has narrowed, while the gap between less-educated immigrants and natives remains significant. College-educated immigrants are often better able to navigate the labor market, not only due to their higher levels of education but also because they are more likely to speak English fluently. On the other hand, less-educated immigrants— who may come from countries where English is not widely spoken—are more likely to face economic challenges, particularly in terms of securing higher-paying jobs.

Moreover, this sorting effect highlights the importance of looking at subgroups within the immigrant population. While the overall wage gap may appear to be narrowing, this trend is driven in part by the fact that more highly educated immigrants are entering the workforce. The average wage for immigrants may still be lower than that of native-born citizens, but this figure can be misleading. When the data is broken down by education level, it becomes clear that the most educated immigrants are doing just as well, if not better, than their native-born counterparts.

ECONOMIC IMPLICATIONS OF EDUCATION AMONG IMMIGRANTS

The growing educational attainment of immigrants has several important economic implications. First, immigrants with higher education levels can fill critical skill gaps in the U.S. labor market. Sectors such as technology, engineering, healthcare, and finance require specialized knowledge, and immigrants with college degrees or advanced training are increasingly providing the expertise needed in these fields. These industries rely heavily on skilled workers, and immigrants have become an integral part of the workforce in these high-demand areas.

In addition to filling skill gaps, highly educated immigrants also contribute to the U.S. economy in other ways. Many educated immigrants go on to become entrepreneurs, creating businesses that generate jobs and contribute to economic growth. Immigrants are more likely to start their own businesses than native-born Americans, and these businesses often have a positive impact on the economy by employing others and generating revenue. The entrepreneurial spirit of educated immigrants has been a key driver of innovation, particularly in industries such as technology and retail.

Moreover, the educational contributions of immigrants extend beyond the workforce. Highly educated immigrants bring new perspectives, ideas, and ways of thinking that enrich the social and cultural fabric of their new country. These individuals often contribute to the development of new technologies, medical advancements, and business strategies, all of which benefit society. Their educational achievements not only help their own families achieve upward mobility but also contribute to the overall prosperity of the nation.

The educational advancement of immigrants is also linked to greater economic competitiveness. Countries that attract and retain highly educated immigrants are better positioned to remain at the forefront of global innovation. Immigrants bring with them diverse skills and knowledge that help drive economic progress. As the global economy becomes increasingly interconnected, the ability to attract skilled workers will become even more important for maintaining a competitive edge.

The educational attainment of immigrants has changed significantly over time, and these changes have important implications for their economic integration. Today, immigrants are among the most highly educated groups to have ever entered the U.S., and this higher level of education has enabled them to contribute more effectively to the economy. However, the relationship between education and earnings is complex, influenced by factors such as English proficiency, credential recognition, and discrimination. Despite these challenges, highly educated immigrants are playing an increasingly important role in the U.S. economy, contributing to innovation, entrepreneurship, and the growth of key industries. As their educational levels continue to rise, immigrants will continue to be an essential part of the U.S. economic landscape.

CHAPTER 4
MARRIAGE, FAMILY STRUCTURE, AND SOCIAL ASSIMILATION

MARRIAGE AND FAMILY DYNAMICS

Marriage and family structure are important considerations for policymakers because of the implications they have for both social assimilation and economic success. The way immigrants form families and the role that marriage plays in their integration into American society are crucial factors in understanding their adaptation to life in the U.S.

Immigrants in the United States tend to marry at higher rates and have larger families than their native-born counterparts. This trend is not necessarily the result of economic prosperity in the U.S. but can largely be attributed to the cultural and societal norms of the countries immigrants come from. In many parts of the world, marriage is seen as an essential step in adulthood, and large families are more common. As a result, immigrants to the U.S. often bring these traditions with them.

In their home countries, marriage and family life may be central aspects of social and cultural identity. In places where extended families are the norm, it is expected that individuals marry young and have children early in life. These customs do not change just because an immigrant moves to a new country. Many immigrants arrive already married and often bring their children or start new families soon after arriving. This continuity of family structure from their countries of origin can sometimes make the transition to life in the U.S. smoother, as the family remains a key point of stability in a new and unfamiliar environment.

Moreover, marriage rates among immigrants are often higher because of the selection effect—the people who choose to immigrate to the U.S. are often those who are already married or have intentions to marry. In other words, immigrants tend to come from backgrounds where marriage is valued, which contributes to the higher marriage rates observed in immigrant populations. The U.S. is seen as a place of opportunity, and many immigrants see marriage to further solidify their chances of long-term success in the country, whether for securing legal status or ensuring a stable family life.

Compared to native-born Americans, immigrants often form families that are larger on average. This is also influenced by cultural norms in their home countries, where larger families are more common. Many immigrants come from cultures where having many children is seen as a source of pride and a way to provide for the future. While economic factors in the U.S. can influence family size, these cultural practices continue to play a significant role in shaping family structure.

CULTURAL INFLUENCE ON FAMILY STRUCTURE

The family structure of immigrants is deeply shaped by the customs and traditions of their home countries. Cultural norms regarding marriage, parenting, and family life tend to follow immigrants across borders and remain significant in the new environment. These practices can sometimes be at odds with mainstream American culture, which often emphasizes smaller family units and later marriages.

For example, in many Latin American, Middle Eastern, and South Asian cultures, it is common for families to live in close-knit extended family structures, where multiple generations may live in the same household. This contrasts with the more individualistic family units often seen in the U.S., where nuclear families (parents and children) are more common. Immigrants may maintain these larger family structures, seeking out communities where other immigrants share similar cultural backgrounds. This creates a sense of community and belonging, but it can also lead to social tensions, especially if larger family units are perceived as unusual or difficult to integrate into American society.

Similarly, in many cultures, marriage is not only a personal decision but a family and community event that involves a broader social network. Immigrant marriages often reflect these deep cultural roots, where families play a significant role in choosing spouses and maintaining social connections. For example, arranged marriages are more common in certain immigrant groups, particularly among those from South Asia and the Middle East. While arranged marriages might seem foreign to mainstream American society, they are a culturally ingrained practice that can influence the family dynamics of immigrant groups.

As immigrants adapt to life in the U.S., some of these cultural norms might be challenged by the different values they encounter. For instance, the American emphasis on individualism and personal freedom might clash with the more collective nature of family life in many immigrant communities. However, despite these challenges, many immigrants continue to maintain strong family bonds, and family remains central to their identity and sense of belonging.

Cultural values surrounding marriage and family also influence the expectations that immigrants have regarding their children. Immigrant parents often place a high value on education and hard work, hoping that their children will succeed in American society. They may also continue to uphold traditional roles within the family, such as strong parental authority, respect for elders, and gender roles, which can differ from the more democratic norms often found in American households. These cultural differences can sometimes create tension between immigrant parents and their children, particularly if the younger generation becomes more assimilated into American culture.

LEGAL AND ECONOMIC FACTORS

Marriage also plays an important role in the legal and economic integration of immigrants. One of the ways in which immigrants can secure permanent residency or citizenship in the U.S. is by marrying a U.S. citizen or permanent resident. The immigration system provides a pathway to legal status for those who marry American citizens, and this legal channel can significantly influence the decision to marry.

In many cases, marriage becomes a practical way for immigrants to solidify their status in the U.S., particularly for those who may not have other means of gaining legal residence. This dynamic is particularly evident among immigrants from countries where economic and political instability makes it difficult to secure permanent residency through employment or other avenues. For these individuals, marriage to a U.S. citizen or permanent resident may offer a more secure and straightforward path to legal status.

While marriage can provide legal and economic benefits, it can also complicate the assimilation process. For example, marriages to

U.S. citizens or permanent residents may create cultural tensions, as immigrants may be encouraged to conform to American societal norms, which can sometimes conflict with their cultural values. Additionally, the legal status of immigrants can be precarious, especially if their marriage is scrutinized by authorities or if they face difficulties in proving the legitimacy of their relationship.

Furthermore, the economic implications of marriage can influence family structure in immigrant communities. Immigrants often face challenges in securing stable employment, and marriage can provide economic support. In some cases, both spouses may work to support the family, leading to a dual-income household. This can be especially important in immigrant communities where wages may be lower than the national average, and larger families may place additional financial pressure on households.

While marriage can provide legal and economic benefits, it can also create economic vulnerabilities. Immigrants who marry solely to gain legal status may face challenges in maintaining stable, long-term relationships. These relationships can be further complicated by the stress of adjusting to life in the U.S. and navigating the complexities of the immigration system.

IMPACT ON SOCIAL INTEGRATION

Marriage and family structure play a significant role in an immigrant's sense of belonging in American society. For many immigrants, family provides a source of stability and identity in a new and often unfamiliar environment. The act of marrying and starting a family in the U.S. can be seen as a commitment to building a life in the country, and the family unit can offer emotional and social support in the face of challenges.

Immigrants who form families in the U.S. are often able to establish stronger connections with their communities. They may find support networks among other immigrants or within ethnic enclaves, where they can share cultural experiences and maintain traditions. These social networks help immigrants to integrate more easily into society and create a sense of belonging.

On the other hand, the presence of large immigrant families can sometimes create social divisions. In areas where immigrant populations are growing rapidly, tensions can arise between immigrant communities and native-born citizens, particularly if there are differences in family structure or cultural practices. In some cases, immigrants may be viewed as resistant to assimilation because of their cultural traditions or family dynamics, leading to stereotyping and discrimination.

Despite these challenges, marriage and family life remain central to the social integration of immigrants. By forming families in the U.S., immigrants not only contribute to the country's demographic growth but also build the social capital that can facilitate long-term integration. The importance of family in immigrant life underscores the fact that social assimilation is not only about economic success but also about emotional and social connections that contribute to a sense of belonging.

Marriage and family structure play a critical role in the social and economic integration of immigrants. Immigrants tend to marry at higher rates and have larger families compared to native-born Americans, largely due to cultural norms and the selection effect of those who choose to immigrate. While marriage provides legal and economic benefits, it can also present challenges, particularly in terms of social assimilation. Cultural differences in family structures, combined with legal and economic factors, influence the way immigrants integrate into American society. Ultimately, marriage and family serve as important pillars of support for immigrants, offering stability and social connections that are vital to their successful integration into U.S. society.

CHAPTER 5
CULTURE ASSIMILATION
AND IDENTITY

CULTURAL PRACTICES AND THE PACE OF ASSIMILATION

Cultural assimilation is a complex and deeply personal process for immigrants in the United States. It involves navigating a new environment, adopting certain customs and traditions, and balancing this with the preservation of one's own cultural identity. As immigrants arrive in the U.S., they encounter a society rich in diversity yet shaped by distinct cultural norms and values.

While some immigrants embrace assimilation as a pathway to opportunity and acceptance, others face the tension of maintaining their heritage in a culture that may not fully understand or accept them.

The speed of cultural assimilation varies widely among immigrant groups, influenced by factors such as the country of origin, linguistic similarity, and societal expectations. For example, immigrants from Western Europe—countries like Ireland, England, and Denmark—historically assimilated more quickly due to cultural and linguistic similarities. On the other hand, immigrants from countries with less cultural alignment, such as Russia, Africa, or China, often experienced a slower process of integration.

Assimilation often begins with visible cultural markers. Immigrants might adopt American holidays like Thanksgiving or the Fourth of July, participate in local traditions, or embrace American cuisine. These practices serve as gateways to forming connections with native-born Americans. However, cultural assimilation is not a one-way process. Many immigrants enrich American society by introducing their traditions, foods, and festivals, contributing to the nation's cultural mosaic.

Despite these adaptations, many immigrants strive to retain elements of their heritage. This delicate balance between assimilation and cultural preservation reflects the complex experience of building a new identity while honoring the old.

NAMES: A SUBTLE INDICATOR OF ASSIMILATION

One subtle yet powerful marker of cultural assimilation is the choice of names for children. Immigrant parents often face a significant decision: should they give their children names that reflect their ethnic heritage or choose names that are more commonly associated with American culture?

For instance, names like Maria or Ahmed often signify strong ties to one's cultural background, while names like Sarah or John may be perceived as more "American." The decision to adopt American-sounding names is not merely cosmetic—it can have social and economic implications. Studies suggest that children with less foreign-sounding names are more likely to succeed academically, secure higher-paying jobs, and face fewer instances of discrimination.

The choice of names, however, is not uniform across all immigrant groups. Historical data shows that Irish and Italian immigrants were among the fastest to adopt American naming agreements, while Eastern Europeans and Russian Jews retained traditional names longer. Regardless of the pace, the shift in naming practices reflects a broader trend of blending into American culture while navigating the pressures of societal acceptance.

THE ECONOMIC AND SOCIAL BENEFITS OF ASSIMILATION

Cultural assimilation offers significant benefits for immigrants, particularly in terms of economic and social integration. Immigrants who learn English, adapt to American customs and understand societal norms often find it easier to access better job opportunities, navigate educational systems, and establish meaningful connections in their communities.

For many, assimilation serves as a bridge to economic stability and upward mobility. Immigrants who successfully integrate into American society often secure higher-paying jobs, achieve financial independence, and contribute to the nation's economy. Second-generation immigrants, in particular, benefit from their parents' efforts, often achieving significant social and economic success compared to their ancestors.

Beyond economics, assimilation fosters social cohesion. Immigrants who participate in American cultural practices— whether by celebrating national holidays or engaging in community activities—help build relationships with native-born citizens. These connections create mutual understanding and reduce barriers that might otherwise divide communities.

Balancing Assimilation with Cultural Identity

While assimilation provides clear advantages, it is not without its challenges. Many immigrants deal with the fear of losing their cultural heritage as they adapt to a new society. For some, cultural traditions serve as an anchor—a way to stay connected to their roots and pass down their identity to future generations.

The tension between assimilation and cultural preservation is particularly pronounced among second-generation immigrants. These individuals often live between two worlds, adopting American customs in public settings while practicing their parents' traditions at home. This duality can create identity challenges but also enrich their sense of self, allowing them to navigate both cultures with ease.

Immigrant communities across the U.S. reflect this balance. Neighborhoods with strong ethnic identities, such as Chinatown or Little Italy, are examples of how immigrants maintain their cultural practices while contributing to the larger American identity. These spaces allow immigrants to celebrate their heritage without feeling pressured to conform entirely to mainstream norms.

Challenges of Cultural Assimilation

Despite its benefits, cultural assimilation can be fraught with difficulties. Immigrants often face societal pressures to conform to American norms, which can feel like a rejection of their own identity. For example, immigrants with accents or those who wear traditional clothing may encounter discrimination or exclusion. These experiences can create a sense of alienation, making it harder for immigrants to feel accepted in their new homes.

Language barriers also pose significant challenges. Immigrants who struggle to learn English may find it difficult to access essential services, secure employment, or build relationships with native-born citizens. This limitation can create a cycle of economic hardship and social isolation.

For many, the process of assimilation involves sacrifices that are not always recognized by the broader society. The pressure to fit in can lead to feelings of loss, as immigrants are forced to navigate a delicate balance between integrating into their new environment and preserving their cultural heritage.

EMBRACING A DUAL IDENTITY

Cultural assimilation is an evolving and deeply personal process. It is not about erasing one's heritage but about finding a way to thrive in a new environment while maintaining connections to the past. Immigrants in the U.S. continually navigate this journey, shaping their own identities and enriching the nation.

As the U.S. becomes increasingly diverse, it is crucial to foster an environment where assimilation is seen not as a demand but as an opportunity. By embracing the unique contributions of immigrant communities and promoting inclusivity, the nation can honor its history as a land of opportunity and diversity.

Cultural assimilation is not a one-size-fits-all experience. It is a mosaic of stories, struggles, and triumphs—a testament to the resilience and adaptability of those who seek a better life while holding on to the traditions that define them.

CHAPTER 6
THE ROLE OF IMMIGRANT COMMUNITIES AND LOCAL SUPPORT SYSTEMS

COMMUNITY AND SUPPORT NETWORKS: A LIFELINE FOR IMMIGRANTS

Immigrating to a new country is a journey filled with hope, challenges, and the need for belonging. For many immigrants, community networks become an essential part of their ability to settle, integrate, and thrive in their new environment. These networks provide emotional support, practical assistance, and a sense of connection that helps immigrants navigate the complexities of starting anew.

For many immigrants, the first challenge is adapting to a new and unfamiliar way of life. The barriers of language, culture, and unfamiliar systems can feel overwhelming. Immigrant communities serve as a bridge, offering guidance and resources that help newcomers overcome these initial challenges.

These networks often form naturally among people who share a common language, culture, or origin. They provide practical help—whether it's finding housing, securing a job, or understanding the legal requirements of residency. Beyond these solid benefits, immigrant communities create a sense of belonging, offering a space where individuals can connect with others who understand their experiences.

In addition to practical support, these networks play an emotional role. Many immigrants face isolation and homesickness as they adjust to their new surroundings. Within their community, they find a reminder of home through shared traditions, foods, and celebrations. These cultural ties are not only comforting but also help immigrants maintain their identities while they integrate into their new environment.

DR. FAKONDO'S ROLE: A COMMUNITY LEADER IN ACTION

One inspiring example of community leadership is Rev. Dr. Victor H. Fakondo, who has become a cornerstone of the Sierra Leonean community in New Jersey. Dr. Fakondo's work reflects the powerful impact that a single individual can have in helping others navigate the immigrant experience.

As a young immigrant from Sierra Leone, Dr. Fakondo faced many of the same struggles that new arrivals encounter, from culture shock to financial hardship. "As a new immigrant, you need a lot of help and advice," says Sydney Brima-Jah, of Edison, a church member who knew Fakondo as a young man in Sierra Leone and sought him out when he moved to New Jersey in 1989. However, his determination to succeed and his commitment to education laid the foundation for a life dedicated to helping others. Today, he is known as a leader, mentor, and activist who provides critical support to his fellow Sierra Leoneans and other immigrants in the area. "Most people say, 'You have to meet Victor,'" Brima-Jah recalls. "If you come to New Jersey, you end up meeting him anyway."

Dr. Fakondo's contributions extend beyond individual acts of kindness. He has welcomed new arrivals, offering them a place to stay, helping them apply for Social Security numbers, and guiding them through the process of finding housing and employment. When there is a death in the family, Fakondo is often the first-person people call. "If you do a favor, that person tells others," Says Fakondo's wife: Viola Fakondo. "It goes so quickly, it's like wildfire." His efforts have not only eased the transition for countless individuals but also strengthened the Sierra Leonean community. Through Fakondo, Brima-Jah, now a U.S. citizen, was introduced to the Sierra Leonean community. "These are the people I love. It is like one big family, especially the church," he says.

IMMIGRANT NETWORKS: PRACTICAL SUPPORT FOR A NEW START

Immigrant communities thrive when they are supported by leaders who understand their unique needs. Leaders like Dr. Fakondo play a key role in creating networks that address these challenges. For instance, he has helped individuals navigate the complexities of immigration paperwork, provided advice on educational opportunities, and even offered financial assistance to those in need. "Some people see him as a leader. Some people view him as someone they can exploit," says friend Jacob Tower, of Maryland. "Only true leaders can do what Victor does. He does not go into it asking, 'What's in it for me?' It is 'How can I help this person?'

These networks also extend into areas such as healthcare, education, and employment. By connecting newcomers with the right resources, community leaders help them establish stable and productive lives. For example, Dr. Fakondo's emphasis on education has inspired many to pursue higher education and professional training, opening doors to better opportunities.

Churches, cultural organizations, and social clubs also serve as hubs for immigrant networks. These spaces provide a platform for members to share information, offer mutual support, and celebrate their cultural heritage. In doing so, they foster a sense of unity and shared purpose that strengthens the entire community.

THE IMPACT OF SOCIAL SUPPORT: A PATHWAY TO INTEGRATION

The support provided by immigrant communities and local organizations extends beyond practical assistance. It plays a crucial role in helping individuals feel a sense of belonging in their new country.

Churches, for example, often serve as more than places of worship. They become gathering spaces where immigrants can connect, share their struggles, and find encouragement. Dr. Fakondo loves the church. A Sunday without church leaves him feeling incomplete and unsatisfied. On family vacations, whether in Hawaii or London, Fakondo finds the nearest church to attend Sunday services.

Dr. Fakondo's involvement with Bethel United Church exemplifies this. His efforts have not only strengthened the Sierra Leonean congregation but have also created a welcoming environment for others seeking a supportive community. A soft-spoken pharmacist and preacher of the gospel, Fakondo is not just a church leader, but also an activist, a mentor, and a social worker. When he gets involved in a community project, he does not attend a few meetings; he becomes the chairperson of the board. "After work, that's when my whole day starts," he says, reflecting his tireless commitment to serving others. Emily Sawyer, Abigail Yatteh, his sisters, and lay leader: Matthew Young at Bethel United, sums it up well: "He's the axle that the wheel is turning on."

Social organizations and mentorship programs further contribute to this sense of belonging. These groups provide opportunities for immigrants to learn new skills, participate in civic life, and give back to their communities. Mentorship has a lasting impact, as experienced individuals like Dr. Fakondo guide newcomers through the challenges of integration. His role extends beyond just advice; he provides practical support and encouragement, drawing from his own experiences to inspire and uplift those who are beginning their journey in a new country.

The benefits of these support systems extend to the broader society as well. Immigrants who feel supported are more likely to engage with their communities, contribute to the local economy, and participate in civic activities. This mutual exchange enriches both the immigrant population and the host society, creating a more inclusive and cohesive community. Dr. Fakondo's dedication to his community serves as an example of how an individual's compassion and leadership can make a profound difference, fostering connections that benefit everyone.

BUILDING STRONGER COMMUNITIES TOGETHER

The role of immigrant communities and local support systems cannot be overstated. They provide the foundation for successful integration, helping newcomers overcome challenges and build fulfilling lives in their new country. Leaders like Rev. Dr. Victor H. Fakondo demonstrate the profound impact that individual dedication and community solidarity can have on the lives of immigrants.

As the U.S. continues to welcome immigrants from around the world, fostering these networks will remain essential. By investing in community resources, supporting mentorship programs, and recognizing the contributions of immigrant leaders, we can create an environment where everyone could thrive.

The journey of immigration is never easy, but with the strength of community and the guidance of compassionate leaders, it becomes a pathway to hope, opportunity, and belonging.

CHAPTER 7
THE IMMIGRANT EXPERIENCE: CHALLENGES AND TRIUMPHS

CHALLENGES FACED BY NEW IMMIGRANTS

Immigrants come to the United States with dreams of creating better lives for themselves and their families. Whether seeking economic opportunities, escaping political unrest, or reuniting with loved ones, their journeys are fueled by hope and determination. However, this pursuit often comes with challenges. Immigrants must navigate an unfamiliar landscape, adapt to new customs, and overcome barriers that can feel insurmountable at times.

The journey to the United States is rarely without obstacles, and immigrants often face a host of challenges that test their resilience. From adjusting to a new culture and language to overcoming financial hardships and discrimination, these hurdles can be intimidating. On top of the emotional strain of leaving their home countries, immigrants must navigate a demanding and unfamiliar environment, which can add to their stress and uncertainty.

One of the most significant challenges immigrants face is culture shock, a feeling of disorientation and discomfort that comes with adapting to a new way of life. This experience can be overwhelming as immigrants strive to find their place in a society with customs and traditions that are often vastly different from their own.

- **Culture Shock:**

For many immigrants, adapting to American culture is one of the first and most overwhelming challenges. Everyday activities that seem simple to native-born citizens—such as shopping for groceries or using public transportation—can be confusing and intimidating for newcomers. The fast-paced nature of American life, with its emphasis on individualism and efficiency, often contrasts sharply with the communal and slower-paced cultures many immigrants come from.

Cultural differences can extend to social norms, etiquette, and expectations. For example, immigrants may struggle to understand the informal, yet professional tone commonly used in American workplaces or the emphasis on punctuality. These adjustments take time, and the initial period of adaptation can feel isolating and overwhelming.

These cultural adjustments often go hand in hand with the challenges of learning a new language. Without fluency, understanding social cues and navigating everyday interactions can become even more difficult, further deepening the sense of isolation and making the transition feel even more overwhelming.

- **Language Barriers:**

A lack of English proficiency is one of the most significant challenges immigrants faces. Without a strong command of the language, tasks like filling out job applications, accessing healthcare, or communicating with teachers about their children's education become daunting. Immigrants often find themselves relegated to low-paying jobs with limited opportunities for advancement simply because they cannot effectively communicate their skills or qualifications.

Even those who speak some English may struggle with regional accents, idioms, or cultural subtleties in communication. This language barrier can worsen feelings of isolation and make it difficult to build relationships with native-born Americans.

The difficulties in communication can also impact job opportunities and income, adding to the financial pressures immigrants face. Without strong language skills, finding stable, well-paying employment can be challenging, making it harder to support themselves and their families.

- **Financial Struggles:**

Financial challenges are nearly universal among immigrants, especially during the initial years in a new country. Many arrive with limited savings and face high living expenses, particularly in urban areas where immigrant communities are often concentrated. Jobs that require little to no English proficiency tend to pay minimum wage, making it difficult for immigrants to cover necessities, let alone save for the future.

Immigrants also send money back to family members in their home countries, further straining their finances. Balancing these responsibilities while trying to establish a stable life in the U.S. can be an immense burden, leading to stress and exhaustion.

These financial challenges are often compounded by the additional stress of discrimination. Immigrants may face biases in the workplace or community, which can limit their job opportunities, affect their income, and add another layer of difficulty to their efforts to build a better life.

- **Discrimination:**

Immigrants often face prejudice and discrimination based on their ethnicity, accent, or appearance. This bias can manifest in the workplace, in schools, or even in public spaces, creating additional barriers to success. Negative stereotypes and xenophobic attitudes can make immigrants feel unwelcome and hinder their ability to integrate into American society.

Despite these challenges, immigrants consistently show remarkable resilience. They draw on their inner strength and the support of their communities to overcome these obstacles and build fulfilling lives in their new homeland.

One powerful example of this resilience is Rev. Dr. Victor H. Facundo's journey. His story embodies the strength and determination that many immigrants draw upon to overcome adversity and create a positive impact in their communities.

DR. FAKONDO'S PERSONAL STORY: AN INSPIRATION OF RESILIENCE

Dr. Victor Fakondo's journey is a powerful example of the immigrant experience, marked by resilience and an unwavering commitment to helping others. Arriving in the U.S. as a young man from Sierra Leone, he faced many of the same challenges that millions of immigrants encounter, including culture shock, financial hardship, and discrimination.

As a Creole-speaking immigrant, Dr. Fakondo struggled a little bit with English, which made him a target for ridicule. "When you come to this country with an accent, they make fun of you. They look at you like you are a fool," Fakondo says.

At one of his first jobs, Fakondo says he left the lab he was working in with a colleague for only a few minutes. When he returned, his books and work had vanished. It was obvious the colleague had disposed of them, but the man denied it.

"I cried," Fakondo says. "How could someone do something like that? It's senseless behavior."

Financial difficulties were another significant hurdle. While studying at Kean University and later at Rutgers, he was getting by with financial aid and living with a cousin in Franklin, often skipping meals to make ends meet. Despite these hardships, he remained focused on his education, understanding that it was the key to a brighter future.

These early struggles shaped Dr. Fakondo's character and inspired him to become a mentor and advocate for other immigrants. By drawing on his own experiences, he has been able to guide and support newcomers, helping them navigate the challenges of starting a new life in the U.S.

SUPPORT AND RESILIENCE: THE POWER OF COMMUNITY

One of the most important factors in overcoming the challenges of immigration is the support of a strong community. Immigrants often form tight-knit networks where they can share resources, provide emotional support, and celebrate their cultural heritage.

Rev. Dr. Fakondo has been a pillar of the Sierra Leonean community in New Jersey. Known for his generosity and willingness to help, he has assisted countless immigrants with practical needs, such as finding housing, filling out paperwork, or securing jobs. His home became a refuge for newcomers, and his phone was always available for those seeking advice or assistance. Fakondo's phone rings at all hours -- a fact confirmed by his wife, with a slight roll of her eyes. Fakondo sleeps four, or five hours a night. "People call me at 2am in the morning because their car broke down," Fakondo says. "I have AAA. I have never used it. It's for them."

In earlier years, there was barely a room in the house because new arrivals found their way to Fakondo. "The house was packed full," recalls the late Audrey Fakondo. "A whole lot of people would live with us. He took them in, not me."

The support immigrants receive from their communities can make a profound difference. Whether it is through religious institutions like Bethel United Church or social organizations, these networks offer a sense of belonging and help newcomers navigate the complexities of American life.

THE IMPORTANCE OF EDUCATION

Education is one of the most powerful tools for overcoming the challenges of immigration. For many immigrants, it serves as a gateway to better opportunities and a more secure future.

Dr. Fakondo has long been an advocate for education, both for himself and for others. He has encouraged countless individuals to pursue higher education, guiding them through the application process and even helping them secure financial aid. His dedication to education inspired him to establish Marie's Allied Health and Technical Institute, which provides training in practical skills like nursing, pharmacy, and other health-related courses.

His late father put education and church more than anything else, and Fakondo is very much his father's son. He has pursued cousins, friends, in-laws, and church members into college, suggesting practical programs such as nursing or computers. If it is a question of money, Fakondo offers help applying for grants or financial aid.

Those Fakondo has nudged into school get weekly phone calls from him. "I give them a little encouragement," he says. "No one called me."

One of the students on Fakondo's call list is Fanta Kallon, of Franklin, a native of one of Sierra Leone's provinces who came to the United States in 1990. With Fakondo's help, Kallon, a single mother raising two boys, became a registered nurse. Fakondo hosted a graduation party for her and then urged her to go back to school and get a bachelor's degree. She has since enrolled at Kean University.

"I would call Victor anytime and he would counsel me on the phone," Kallon says. "He's a father, a brother, an uncle. You can call him anytime. It does not matter what time of day. No matter what the situation, he'll work hard to help."

Through education, immigrants can break free from cycles of poverty and achieve upward mobility. They gain the skills and knowledge needed to access higher-paying jobs, contribute to their communities, and provide a better future for their families.

TRIUMPHS AMID CHALLENGES

Despite the difficulties they face, immigrants often emerge stronger and more determined. Their stories are filled with examples of perseverance and success. Second-generation immigrants, in particular, often achieve significant upward mobility, benefiting from the sacrifices and hard work of their parents.

Dr. Fakondo's story is a testament to the triumphs that can emerge from adversity. From a young man struggling to adapt to a new culture, he became a respected pharmacist, a community leader, and an advocate for education and social justice. His journey demonstrates the incredible potential of immigrants to overcome challenges and make meaningful contributions to society.

TURNING CHALLENGES INTO ACHIEVEMENTS

The immigrant experience in the United States is a testament to the resilience of the human spirit. While the journey is often tense with obstacles, immigrants find ways to adapt, grow, and thrive.

Dr. Fakondo's story highlights the importance of community support, education, and perseverance in overcoming the challenges of immigration. By sharing his experiences and helping others, he has not only built a successful life for himself but also empowered countless individuals to do the same.

As the U.S. continues to welcome immigrants, it is essential to recognize their contributions and address the barriers they face. By fostering a more inclusive and supportive environment, we can ensure that the immigrant journey remains one of hope, opportunity, and triumph.

CHAPTER 8
THE ROLE OF CHURCHES AND RELIGIOUS INSTITUTIONS

BETHEL UNITED CHURCH: A PILLAR OF THE SIERRA LEONEAN COMMUNITY

For many immigrants, adjusting to a new country can be overwhelming. They face cultural, linguistic, and emotional challenges while trying to establish themselves in an unfamiliar environment. In this context, churches and other religious institutions often become lifelines, providing support, community, and spiritual grounding.

Religious institutions play a unique role in helping immigrants navigate the complexities of life in a new land. They are not just places of worship but also hubs for socialization, resource-sharing, and community building. In the U.S., churches like Bethel United Church have been instrumental in fostering connections among immigrant populations, offering a sense of belonging and practical assistance.

Bethel United Church, the first African church in its area, serves as a cornerstone for the Sierra Leonean community in New Jersey. For many immigrants, the church is a sanctuary where they can find comfort, understanding, and guidance. It acts as a bridge between their past and present, providing a space where traditions from their home country are preserved while fostering integration into American society.

The church is more than a place for Sunday worship. It offers immigrants opportunities to connect with others who share similar experiences. Through fellowship events, choir practices, and community gatherings, Bethel United helps immigrants build relationships that go beyond religious ties. These connections create a network of support that extends into everyday life.

The church also plays a practical role in addressing the challenges immigrants face. From helping newcomers find housing to providing referrals for jobs, Bethel United acts as a community resource center. Its programs, such as English language classes and mentorship initiatives, empower individuals to overcome barriers and achieve their goals.

The Bethel United's impact is evident in the stories of countless individuals who have found solace and strength within its walls.

Dr. Fakondo's Leadership: A Catalyst for Community Building

At the heart of Bethel United Church's success is the tireless dedication of leaders like Dr. Victor Fakondo. As a Sierra Leonean immigrant who once faced the same challenges as many of his peers, Dr. Fakondo has made it his mission to support others on their journey. His involvement in the church reflects his deep commitment to creating a strong and unified community.

One of Dr. Fakondo's most significant contributions is his ability to inspire others to act. Through his leadership, he has encouraged the congregation to expand its outreach efforts, ensuring that the church remains a symbol of hope for all who enter. His efforts have strengthened the Sierra Leonean community and set a standard for leadership that blends compassion with action.

Church members often describe Dr. Fakondo as the glue that holds the community together. As one member put it, "He's not just a leader; he's a father, a mentor, and a friend to everyone who needs him."

FAITH AS A PILLAR OF ASSIMILATION

Religious institutions like Bethel United Church do more than provide spiritual support; they help immigrants navigate the process of assimilation. Faith offers a sense of stability and purpose, enabling individuals to cope with the uncertainties of their new environment.

For many immigrants, participating in church activities is a way to practice new cultural norms in a safe and supportive setting. From learning to communicate effectively in English to understanding American social customs, the church provides a platform for gradual adaptation.

Churches also encourage civic engagement, teaching immigrants about their rights and responsibilities as members of their new communities. They often organize voter registration drives, workshops on local laws, and volunteer opportunities that help individuals integrate into broader society.

At the same time, religious institutions help immigrants retain their cultural identity. Services and events that incorporate traditional music, language, and customs allow members to stay connected to their roots while embracing their new home. This balance between preservation and adaptation is a cornerstone of successful assimilation.

THE BROADER IMPACT OF RELIGIOUS INSTITUTIONS

The influence of churches like Bethel United extends beyond their congregations. By fostering strong and cohesive communities, they contribute to the social and economic fabric of the larger society. Immigrants who feel supported are more likely to engage in civic life, start businesses, and participate in local initiatives, enriching their neighborhoods and beyond.

Religious institutions also promote understanding and collaboration among diverse groups. Interfaith events, cultural celebrations, and charity drives bring people from different backgrounds together, fostering mutual respect and shared goals. These interactions break down stereotypes and build bridges between immigrant and native-born populations.

The broader impact of these efforts is a more inclusive society where diversity is celebrated, and everyone can thrive.

A SOURCE OF STRENGTH AND UNITY

The role of churches and religious institutions in the lives of immigrants cannot be exaggerated. They provide more than spiritual guidance—they are centers for socialization, support, and community building. Through their programs and initiatives, they help immigrants navigate the challenges of assimilation while preserving their cultural identities.

Rev. Dr. Victor Fakondo's leadership at Bethel United Church exemplifies the transformative power of these institutions. His dedication to serving others has strengthened his community and inspired countless individuals to overcome obstacles and achieve their dreams.

As the U.S. continues to welcome immigrants from around the world, the role of religious institutions will remain vital. By fostering connections, offering practical support, and promoting a sense of belonging, they create pathways to integration and success.

The journey of immigration is never easy, but with the strength of faith and the guidance of compassionate leaders, it becomes a story of hope, resilience, and unity.

CHAPTER 9
IMMIGRANTS AND CIVIC ENGAGEMENT

COMMUNITY LEADERSHIP: DR. FAKONDO'S ROLE

Dr. Victor Fakondo stood at the heart of his community, a living testament to the power of leadership and resilience. As an immigrant who arrived in the United States under challenging circumstances, his journey to becoming a prominent figure in New Jersey's immigrant advocacy was anything but linear. His work extended beyond the typical boundaries of community service; he embodied the essence of a leader whose actions spoke louder than words.

Dr. Fakondo's days were often packed with activity—visiting community centers, attending board meetings, or organizing rallies to shed light on immigrant struggles. His ability to balance these responsibilities while fostering meaningful connections with those around him set him apart as a trusted and respected leader. "He doesn't just talk about change; he works for it," said a fellow board member of the New Jersey Immigrant Policy Network, an organization he helped elevate through relentless advocacy.

The driving force behind his efforts was a deep understanding of the immigrant experience. He had once walked the same uncertain path as those he now helped, navigating a foreign land with limited resources. His empathy and determination to give back made him an anchor in his community.

ADVOCACY AND SOCIAL CHANGE

One of Dr. Fakondo's notable contributions was his work with the New Jersey Immigrant Policy Network, where he led initiatives that directly impacted the lives of refugees and immigrants. His advocacy went beyond writing policy recommendations; he visited detention centers to meet refugees, ensuring their voices were heard in spaces where they often felt invisible.

During the crisis in Sierra Leone, he organized protests in Washington, D.C., to raise awareness about the devastating impacts of the civil war. These demonstrations brought together a diverse group of advocates, from students to seasoned policymakers, united in the call for justice and support for those fleeing violence.

His work didn't end with protests. Dr. Fakondo became a frequent presence in legislative halls, advocating for reforms to make the immigration system more humane and accessible. "It's not just about policies," he often said. "It's about people—families, children, and communities." His tireless efforts paved the way for greater understanding between immigrants and policymakers, fostering a dialogue that emphasized shared humanity.

BALANCING ACT: SACRIFICES AND COMMITMENTS

While his contributions were immense, they came at a personal cost. Dr. Fakondo's late wife, Audrey, sometimes struggled with the demands placed on her husband. Working late-night shifts as a nurse, she often found their interactions reduced to brief exchanges during weekends. "He's always on the move," she admitted, both proud and wistful. "But I know his work matters, not just to us but to so many families." She said,

The Fakondos' story illustrates the sacrifices that often accompany a life dedicated to advocacy. Despite the challenges, their mutual support underscored the strength of their partnership, rooted in shared values and an unyielding commitment to their community.

BUILDING A LEGACY: THE HEAD START PROGRAM

Dr. Fakondo's journey with the Somerset Community Action Program (SCAP) is a testament to his ability to turn vision into reality. Fakondo, who once lived in poverty himself, began his involvement with SCAP through its policy council—a Head Start-mandated group that includes parents in decision-making. Within months, he was elected council president. Later, he joined SCAP's board of trustees and eventually became its president, leading the agency through a period of rapid growth.

Under his leadership, SCAP expanded dramatically, evolving from a modest operation into an organization that owned three schools and doubled its enrollment. A crowning achievement during this tenure was the $4.1 million Head Start project, largely funded by a federal grant. In 2003, Dr. Fakondo had the honor of breaking ground for the new facility, which would become a cornerstone of SCAP's mission.

Head Start focuses on providing health, nutrition, and early education to preschool-age children from families living at or below the poverty line—defined as $9,000 annually for one parent and a child. "In Somerset County, that's dirt-poor," notes SCAP's executive director, Isaac Dorsey. For these families, the program represents a lifeline, offering essential resources and support that pave the way to a brighter future.

Walking through the newly built facility, Dr. Fakondo often marveled at its significance. "This isn't just a building," he reflected. "It's a symbol of what we can achieve when we work together." His leadership turned SCAP into a model of community action, and his own story serves as proof of its impact. "Do you realize what that means?" asks Dorsey. "That's what we call a Head Start success story."

Although Fakondo no longer serves as SCAP's board president, he remains on the board and has now embarked on his most ambitious project yet: a health and technology institute. This new initiative embodies his lifelong commitment to empowering others through practical training and education, opening doors to success and security.

THE IMPORTANCE OF CIVIC INVOLVEMENT

Dr. Fakondo deeply believed in civic engagement's power to bridge divides and strengthen communities. "Immigrants aren't just beneficiaries," he often reminded his peers. "We are contributors, leaders, and changemakers." His words resonated in a society that often underestimated the potential of immigrant populations.

From organizing voter registration drives to hosting workshops on civic responsibilities, he encouraged others to take active roles in shaping their communities. These efforts empowered individuals to view themselves not as outsiders but as integral members of their new homeland.

Civic involvement also served as a pathway to assimilation. By participating in local initiatives, immigrants found opportunities to connect with their neighbors and navigate societal norms. Dr. Fakondo saw this as a two-way process: while immigrants adapted to their new environment, they also enriched it with their unique perspectives and talents.

STRENGTHENING SOCIAL COHESION

Dr. Fakondo's story was one of resilience and transformation, but it also highlighted the broader impact of immigrant participation in civic life. Through his leadership and advocacy, he fostered a sense of belonging among those who often felt marginalized. His work demonstrated that when immigrants are given the tools and opportunities to engage, they not only improve their own lives but also contribute to the well-being of society.

As he stood before a crowd at one of his many events, he often concluded with the same words: "Together, we are stronger. Together, we build a future where everyone belongs." Those words captured the essence of his mission—a vision of unity, empowerment, and hope.

CHAPTER 10
BUILDING FOR THE FUTURE:
DR. FAKONDO'S VISION

Dr. Victor Fakondo's life is a vivid example of how one person's vision can transform not just individuals but entire communities. His journey from humble beginnings to a position of leadership is marked by resilience, compassion, and an unwavering commitment to empowering others. Today, his efforts culminate in his latest and most ambitious project: **Marie's Allied Health and Technical Institute**, a beacon of hope for immigrants and underprivileged communities.

MARIE'S ALLIED HEALTH AND TECHNICAL INSTITUTE

Named after his mother, Marie's Allied Health and Technology Institute is more than just an educational facility; it is the embodiment of Dr. Fakondo's lifelong mission. Situated in Franklin Township, the institute provides practical education and training in fields such as nursing assistance, pharmacy technology, CPR, Dental Assistants, Central Sterile Technicians, EKG Technicians, Phlebotomy, Medical Billing & Coding, Medical Assistants Training GED, and computer literacy. These programs are carefully designed to equip immigrants and others with skills that can lead to stable, well-paying jobs.

The institute's establishment represents a significant expansion of Dr. Fakondo's work, not only on scale but in scope. By addressing the specific needs of immigrants—many of whom arrive with limited formal education or transferable skills—he aims to bridge gaps that often leave them vulnerable. As Dr. Fakondo explains, "This is about more than teaching skills. It's about opening doors to opportunity and showing people their true potential.

THE VISION BEHIND THE INSTITUTE

Marie's Allied Health and Technology Institute stands out for its focus on practicality and accessibility. Recognizing the financial constraints many immigrants face, Dr. Fakondo has worked tirelessly to keep tuition affordable and secure scholarships for those in need. "Education should never be out of reach for those who need it most," he insists.

Courses at the institute are tailored to the demands of the job market, ensuring graduates are well-positioned to find employment. For instance, the nursing assistant program addresses a growing demand in the healthcare sector, while computer literacy classes empower students to navigate an increasingly digital world. By combining these offerings, the institute provides a pathway to immediate job opportunities and long-term career growth.

THE FUTURE OF IMMIGRANT ASSIMILATION

Dr. Fakondo's vision extends far beyond the walls of the institute. He envisions a future where immigrants are not only assimilated into American society but are also celebrated for their contributions. "Immigrants bring with them a wealth of knowledge, skills, and culture," he says. "Our challenge is to create systems that allow them to thrive."

He advocates an approach to assimilation that balances adaptation with cultural preservation. To this end, the institute often hosts community events where students and their families can share their traditions, fostering a sense of belonging while building bridges with the larger community.

LEGACY AND LONG-TERM IMPACT

Dr. Fakondo's work is centered on empowerment. From his early days with SCAP to his current endeavors, he has consistently sought to uplift others through education, mentorship, and community building. The institute is the latest expression of this commitment, but he sees it as just the beginning.

He hopes to inspire the next generation of leaders, particularly among the immigrant community. By providing not only education but also mentorship, he aims to cultivate individuals who will continue his work and expand its impact. "Legacy isn't about what you achieve," he reflects. "It's about what you inspire others to achieve."

GLOBAL CONNECTIONS: EXTENDING THE IMPACT TO SIERRA LEONE

While much of Dr. Fakondo's work focuses on the United States, his heart remains deeply connected to Sierra Leone, the country of his birth. He views his success in the U.S. as a foundation for greater change back home. "I want to help folks here, but if God gives me a long life, I want to go home and help there," he shares.

Dr. Fakondo dreams of establishing a similar institute in Sierra Leone, one that addresses the unique challenges faced by the country. From healthcare training to vocational programs, he hopes to create opportunities that will empower his fellow Sierra Leoneans to rebuild and thrive. "Maybe this can be a stepping stone to move on and do even better things there," he says with quiet determination.

A New Chapter, A Continuing Mission

At the helm of Marie's Allied Health and Technology Institute, Dr. Fakondo's mission has entered a new chapter. Yet, his core values remain unchanged. He continues to champion the belief that education is the key to unlocking human potential and that communities are strongest when they work together.

As he often says, "Building a future isn't just about constructing walls or teaching skills—it's about creating hope. It's about showing people what's possible." Through his work, Dr. Fakondo not only builds futures but also inspires others to dream bigger and reach higher.

CONCLUSION
THE ONGOING PROCESS
OF ASSIMILATION

The journey of assimilation is one of transformation—not just for immigrants but for the societies they join. This process, which evolves over time, is a mutual exchange that benefits both the newcomers and the host community. It is shaped by challenges, triumphs, and the contributions of individuals like Dr. Victor Fakondo, whose life exemplifies the power of resilience, community, and visionary leadership.

THE EVOLVING NATURE OF ASSIMILATION

Assimilation is not a singular event but a continuous process. For immigrants, it means adapting to the norms, language, and customs of their new country while preserving the essence of their cultural identities. For host societies, it involve embracing diversity and creating pathways for inclusion. This delicate balance fosters a dynamic exchange where both parties grow, learn, and enrich each other.

Dr. Fakondo's journey shows that assimilation is not about losing one's identity but about blending it into a broader mosaic. His ability to navigate multiple worlds—maintaining his Sierra Leonean roots while becoming a pillar of his American community—demonstrates that assimilation can be a process of mutual enrichment.

As the United States continues to welcome immigrants from diverse backgrounds, it must acknowledge that assimilation is not one-sided. It requires openness, dialogue, and policies that recognize the value of diversity. This evolving process strengthens the social fabric, creating a society that is both inclusive and cohesive.

FUTURE CHALLENGES AND OPPORTUNITIES

The road to assimilation is not without obstacles. Immigrants face barriers such as discrimination, language struggles, and economic hardship. At the same time, host communities often grapple with misunderstandings and resistance to change. Addressing these challenges requires deliberate action and forward-thinking policies.

Inclusive immigration policies are essential for fostering understanding and integration. Language programs, access to education, and support networks can bridge gaps and create opportunities for immigrants to thrive. At the same time, public awareness campaigns can dispel stereotypes and highlight the contributions of immigrant communities.

Technology and globalization offer new opportunities to support assimilation. Online platforms can connect immigrants to resources, language tools, and professional networks, accelerating their integration into society. Moreover, fostering cross-cultural exchanges through community events and initiatives can build empathy and understanding.

Dr. Fakondo's health and technology institute is an example of how future challenges can be turned into opportunities. By equipping immigrants with practical skills, he not only empowers individuals but also strengthens the communities they serve. His work underscores the importance of education and mentorship as tools for integration and upward mobility.

FINAL REFLECTIONS ON DR. FAKONDO'S WORK

Dr. Victor Fakondo's life is a testament to the possibilities of assimilation when guided by purpose and perseverance. His journey, from a young man navigating the uncertainties of immigration to a leader inspiring change, exemplifies the ideals of integration and community building.

Through his advocacy, education initiatives, and commitment to service, Dr. Fakondo has laid a blueprint for others to follow. He shows that success is not just about personal achievements but about lifting others along the way. His ability to bridge cultural divides and create opportunities for his community highlights the profound impact that one individual can have.

As Dr. Fakondo himself reflects, assimilation is not about forgetting where you come from, it is about using your roots to grow in new soil. His vision for immigrant integration extends beyond his immediate community, reaching back to Sierra Leone and forward to future generations. He inspires others to see the potential within themselves and to work together to create a more inclusive and equitable society.

A VISION FOR THE FUTURE

As we look ahead, the process of assimilation will continue to evolve. The challenges will remain, but so will the opportunities to create a better, more inclusive world. Dr. Fakondo's story reminds us that assimilation is not just about adapting, it is about contributing, connecting, and building a legacy.

Immigrants bring with them the richness of their cultures, the strength of their resilience, and the dreams of a brighter future. By embracing these gifts, societies can grow stronger, more innovative, and more united. The ongoing process of assimilation is a journey worth investing in, for it holds the promise of shared progress and prosperity.

Together, we can build a world where everyone belongs, where differences are celebrated, and where the contributions of immigrants are recognized as essential threads in the fabric of humanity. This vision, exemplified by Dr. Fakondo's life and work, is one of hope, unity, and endless possibility.

www.ingramcontent.com/pod-product-compliance
Lightning Source LLC
Chambersburg PA
CBHW052120030426
42335CB00025B/3071